IN SICKNESS & IN HEALTH

ROBERT C. ROBINSON III, MD
KARLA L. ROBINSON, MD

Love Clones Publishing
www.lcpublishing.net

Printed in the United States of America

First Printing, 2015

ISBN: 978-0-692-38826-6

King James Version Scripture quotations marked "KJV" are taken from the Holy Bible, King James Version (Public Domain).

New International Version Scripture quotations marked (NIV) are taken from the Holy Bible, New International Version®, NIV®.
Copyright © 1973, 1978, 1984 by Biblica, Inc.™
Used by permission of Zondervan. All rights reserved worldwide.

New American Standard Bible
Scripture quotations marked "NASB" are taken from the New American Standard Bible®, Copyright © 1960, 1962, 1963, 1968, 1971, 1972, 1973, 1975, 1977, 1995 by The Lockman Foundation. Used by permission.

New King James Version
Scripture quotations marked "NKJV" are taken from the New King James Version. Copyright © 1982 by Thomas Nelson, Inc. Used by permission. All rights reserved.

New Living Translation
Scripture quotations marked (NLT) are taken from the Holy Bible, New Living Translation, copyright © 1996, 2004, 2007 by Tyndale House Foundation. Used by

permission of Tyndale House Publishers, Inc., Carol
Stream, Illinois 60188.

Publishers:
Love Clones Publishing
Dallas, TX 75205
www.lcpublishing.net

DEDICATION

This book is dedicated to our Fab Four:

Laila, Robbie, Micah, and Avery.

You are our inspiration.

We love you!

ACKNOWLEDGEMENTS

A very special thanks to our family for always supporting our vision to take our health and wellness ministry global! We love you!

To our Pastors, thank you for always speaking greatness over us and for helping us to birth our ministry. We love you!

To our friends, prayer partners, and the entire Have Life family, thank you for your prayers, encouragement, and support. We love you!

TABLE OF CONTENTS

Foreword...**9**

Introduction:
Knowing is Half the Battle......................................**14**

Chapter 1:
You Are What You Eat...**21**

Chapter 2:
Ain't No Mountain High Enough:
Overcoming the Barriers...**32**

Chapter 3:
Your Health is Your Wealth....................................**47**

Chapter 4:
Head of the Household:
Men's Health Matters...**59**

Chapter 5:
Rest, Release, Recharge:
A Woman's Guide to Health....................................**79**

Chapter 6:
Leading By Example:
Raising Healthy Children.......................................**94**

Chapter 7:
Faith and Medicine...**104**

Chapter 8:
Too Blessed To Be Stressed.......................................**116**

Chapter 9:
Fit to Win...**128**

FOREWORD

Initially, seeing the title In Sickness and In Health, one might relegate this book to being about marriage counseling. You know, "for better or for worse, richer or poorer, in sickness and in health..." Funny thing is, as a pastor, I have had many couples repeat these sacred vows before God and a congregation of witnesses, but no one anticipates living through the worse, the poorer and the sickness! An imaginative mind would go further and feel as if this is a book about the trouble surrounding being married with a sick or terminally ill spouse. But the truth is, these pages are filled with more than a discussion on how to survive, it teaches us how to come alive.

Revealed in the pages to come are the secrets to sustainable success as Drs. Robinson teach us "Your

Health is Your Wealth." In Sickness and In Health is a book that stands on the premise that a major shift is occurring as spirituality invades the academy of medicine. While faith and fact wage war over the supreme claim of our health, Drs. Robinson reveal that it no longer has to be either or, but both are possible. Uniquely positioned as licensed, board-certified medical doctors and ordained elders in the Christian faith, they have embraced the Kingdom call to lead this charge. The conflation of medicine and ministry is needed in today's society. With documented research, they delve into the power of prayer as an assisting agent for medical change. They also tackle the barriers we face while attempting to improve our health all while providing scriptures to help the reader strengthen their belief in Jehovah-Rophi (the God that heals).

Years before these thoughts went to print, the

seed of medical ministry was evident in their conversation and way of life. Always willing to offer sound advice and conclude with prayer that encouraged the desperate, they added faith to the weary and brought a bedside manner of care and concern. We see this through the prayers offered at the end of each chapter, as they lead each reader to God's throne for a personal encounter.

Being community leaders has also afforded them to have an amalgam of experience in handling pressing questions concerning subjects such as men's health, leading your children to a healthy lifestyle and how women can recharge themselves back to peace and health. As family medicine and internal medicine practitioners, their experience is far reaching. Even with a thorough understanding of the fact that illness knows no boundaries, they are able to skillfully convey that healthy living is an available opportunity all can seize. For instance, tackling the true reason why men refuse to go to the doctor is not for the faint of heart. Their revelation of "indifference" helps men and those who love them address hidden issues and needs.

Let's be honest, who wants to hear from perfect people attempting to relate to the 99% of us who struggle? Have you looked at magazine covers lately? The persons depicted on the front look nothing like they are shown. Unfortunately, Photoshop is not readily available for real life. This is precisely why In Sickness and In Health was written. Real people living a real life. Drs. Rob and Karla share their personal stories to demonstrate their ability to communicate in a scholarly manner while still being relevant. They are just like the rest of us, working hard to achieve and maintain health. With God's help and the medical revelations offered hereafter, we will all live a successful life. Amongst a myriad of misleading information, their marriage to ministry and medicine

is a blessing to the world.

Shomari L. White Sr.
Pastor and Founder
Have Life Church

INTRODUCTION

KNOWING IS HALF THE BATTLE

Getting wisdom is the most important thing you can do! And with your wisdom, develop common sense and good judgment.
Proverbs 4:7 (TLB)

I n 2000, we made our vows before God and man to love, honor, and cherish one another in sickness and in health. By 2010, we were ready to make a change. After years of living in *sickness*, we were ready to live in *health*. The journey we would embark upon involved a radical leap of faith and a belief that there was more to life than what we had experienced and accepted.

Dr. Karla: After receiving a diagnosis of diabetes at the age of 15, I accepted the fact that I would have to live with this illness and its complications for a lifetime. With an insulin pump, pills, four insulin shots a day, 6-8 finger sticks a day to check my blood sugar, living in sickness over the years was so routine that I hadn't really given a second thought as to whether or not I had a choice to live better.

That all changed, during a season of prayer and fasting, when God gave me the revelation that He desired more for me. It was during this time that I came to realize I wasn't living my best life and that I actually had a say in the matter!

Dr. Rob: I accepted being overweight and the health complications that accompany obesity. Tipping the scales at 225 pounds and only 5' 7" tall, I was developing the beginning stages of pre-

hypertension, glucose intolerance, and obstructive sleep apnea. But I still didn't take the time to make my health a priority.

It wasn't until the birth of our second child that I came to the realization that if I stayed on the course I was on, I wouldn't be around to enjoy our children's lives. It was also at this time that I became active in ministry and realized that God expected more of me.

As husband and wife, we found ourselves partners in love, life, parenting, ministry, and business. As our love continued to grow over the years, so did our family. As our family continued to grow, so did our waistlines. Before we knew it, we were overweight, unhealthy, and testing the very vows we made to love, honor, and cherish one another...in sickness!

You may be wondering how as physicians we found ourselves so unhealthy. The answer is simple...knowing is half the battle. With all of our years of medical schooling and training we knew what the basic principles of health looked like. Of course you have to eat "right," exercise, and get a good night's sleep. But something was still missing.

Yes, as physicians we knew that a healthy lifestyle and a healthy diet were the keys to our healing and living an abundant life. We knew the steps that we needed to take to achieve it. Consequently, we had to use good judgment and common sense to put that knowledge into action.

After a renewing of our minds and a transformation in our lifestyle and eating habits, we are now a combined 100 pounds lighter. We are living healthy, taking no medications, and experiencing abundant life! We are living proof that through fasting, prayer, faith, and a commitment to going through the process, you can change the very course of your lives.

So we fasted and petitioned our God about this, and he answered our prayer.
Ezra 8:23 (NIV)

We wrote *In Sickness and In Health* as an inspirational guide for couples, like us, who are seeking to live their best and healthiest lives. It is a peek into the very journey of discovery we took to reclaim our own health after years of living with sickness and disease. By using biblical principles combined with our medical knowledge and experiences, in this book you'll find insight into the God-given mandate to prosper in health, just as the soul prospers. (3 John 1:2)

There is no one formula for "living in health" that works for everyone. But what is universal is the fact that God desires for you to be healthy. If you need to reclaim your health, first start by asking Him how to do it. Let Him show you the barriers in your lives that are preventing you from experiencing your best

health.

**_Getting wisdom is the most important thing
you can do! And with your wisdom, develop
common sense, and good judgment._**
Proverbs 4:7 (TLB)

Let Him tell you what changes you need to make

in your diet, lifestyle, and/or relationship with Him.

For us, it was too many processed foods, no exercise,

and an overly busy lifestyle. For you, it may be that

you're too stressed, an emotional eater, or not getting

enough sleep. Perhaps it's a poor habit like eating too

infrequently, or maybe you're holding on to the pain

of the past, resentment, or guilt. Seeking God through

fasting and prayer was fundamental to success on our

road to good health. Let Him show you where to start.

**_Show me the right path, O Lord;
point out the road for me to follow._**
Psalm 25:4 (NLT)

On the pages that follow, you'll find the additional steps and biblical inspiration we used to take back our health. Our prayer is that through reading *In Sickness and in Health*, praying together, and using the Word of God as your guide, you too will find the motivation to make those necessary changes in your lives. Congratulations on taking the first steps on your journey from living in sickness to living in health!

CHAPTER 1

YOU ARE WHAT YOU EAT

Taste and see that the Lord is good.
Oh, the joys of those who take refuge in him!
Psalm 34:8 (NLT)

Many times we've heard the phrase "You are what you eat." But how many of us can say we really *know* what we're eating? Although it has been nearly 20 years since nutritional fact labels were added to food packaging, according to the food and beverage industry research conducted by NPD Group's *National Eating Trends®* service, less than 50% of people ever read them. If we "are what we eat," then more than half of us are facing an identity crisis as it relates to our nutritional well-being.

What makes this identity crisis even more troubling is the fact that the vast majority of chronic illnesses today are diet and lifestyle related. This includes obesity, diabetes, hypertension, heart disease, and even some cancers. Some simple, yet profound changes in the foods you eat and the lifestyle choices you make have the potential to alter the course of your life and health. You just have to make it a priority.

Challenge yourself to start paying more attention to your diet by reading nutritional labels and educating yourself on what you are eating and how much you are eating. Oftentimes, we go about our busy day consuming calories, without even realizing it. How many times a day do you go by your pantry at home, the break room at work, or a vending machine while out and grab a "little snack?" If you don't know the answer to this question, then you are not alone. In fact, most researchers believe that people tend to underestimate how much they eat in a day by more than 30% on average.

In the book *Mindless Eating* by Brian Wansink, he and his team of researchers found that this underestimation is even more profound the more you eat. They found that the larger the meal, the more likely we are to underestimate the calorie content of the meal. In one study, people consistently assumed a large meal containing roughly 1,780 calories only contained about 1,000 calories or so. These discrepancies were evident in the estimations of most people - overweight, normal weight, dieticians, nutritionists, and even those in the healthcare field.

The solution to this is becoming proficient in reading food labels. Even as physicians counseling patients daily on their health and how to live a healthy lifestyle, we were once guilty of an identity crisis. We had no idea what we were eating. Often eating more than 1,500 calories *per meal*, as opposed to aiming for the recommended value of 1,800-2,000 calories *per day*; unknowingly, we were on the path of destruction we often counseled our patients against.

After consistently monitoring everything we were eating for just three days, we were in shock and ready to make a change. Once you take stock of how much you are truly eating, it may stop you in your tracks and cause you to make some necessary changes in your diet too.

Reading nutritional facts on a food item can be tricky and a little misleading if you aren't familiar with the format. In fact, there are changes coming to the format of the labeling in 2018 to make it easier to read. But for simplicity's sake, here are a few basic things to focus on.

When reading any food label, the first thing to do is to look at *serving size* and *servings per container.* You have to use these numbers together to know what you are really eating. The rest of the nutritional facts are usually listed *per serving,* so you have to know if the entire food package contains just one serving or more. There is a BIG difference between per serving and per package.

Let's look at an example...

A small bag of chips may not look like a lot of calories at first. The total calories on the label may read 250 calories. A snack with just 250 calories certainly seems reasonable to curb the mid-day hunger craving. However, the calories are always listed *per serving* and oftentimes those small bags of chips may contain two servings or more! Now we see that 250 calorie snack is truthfully a 500 calorie snack, and all of the other nutritional values listed like sodium, carbohydrates, and fat content need to be doubled as well. It's easy to be fooled if not paying close attention.

The label will typically show the amount of fats, carbohydrates; and other nutrients such as protein, fiber, vitamins & minerals as recommended daily value percentages. These values are based on a standard 2,000 or 2,500 calorie per day diet as set by the Food & Drug Administration (FDA). However, these dietary requirements are not the same for everyone.

Sometimes medical restrictions may call for a modified diet. Some common restrictions include calorie restriction for those needing to lose weight, sodium restriction for those following a heart healthy diet or a renal (kidney) diet, or it may be necessary to do carbohydrate restriction for those needing better blood sugar control. If you are unsure if you should follow the guidelines for a regular 2,000 calorie per day diet, you need to speak with your physician.

As spouses, being on one accord as it relates to nutrition is important. If only one of you is intent on having a healthy diet and the other is not, there are going to be constant battles in the kitchen. In reality, the one who does the grocery shopping is always going to be in control. Make sure you have an honest discussion with one another about the importance of a healthy diet and maintaining a healthy weight, and the steps you *both* must take to get there.

As it is in the natural sense, so it is in the spiritual sense. You are what you eat! Are you feeding your spirit man the meat of the Word of God on a regular basis? Or are you facing a spiritual identity crisis by not knowing what to feed your soul?

Just as we need to rid our pantry of the "junk food" that has no nutritional value in an effort to feed the body what it needs to thrive, we need to rid our lives of the "junk" we tend to feast on that keeps us from growing and thriving spiritually. Remember to crave God daily. Taste and see that He is good!

The family that prays together...

Lord, thank you for reminding us of who we are. We are your people and you are our God. We are a chosen people, called by you, and are special and precious in your eyes.

We are ready for change. We no longer accept not knowing what we are feeding our bodies. We are intentional about treating our bodies like the temples you created them to be. Help us to exercise the fruit of the spirit and remember to have self-control when we are eating.

We cancel any diet related diseases and their complications. We don't accept obesity, high blood pressure, diabetes, high cholesterol, kidney disease, cancer, or any other chronic diseases inhabiting our bodies.

Thank you for a fresh start in our diets. Help us to

support one another, believe in one another, and pray for one another to reach the goals we have set. In Jesus' mighty name, Amen.

WORD to live by...

Getting wisdom is the most important thing you can do! And with your wisdom, develop common sense and good judgment.

Proverbs 4:7 (TLB)

But you are a chosen people, a royal priesthood, a holy nation, God's special possession, that you may declare the praises of him who called you out of darkness into his wonderful light.

1 Peter 2:9 (NIV)

Whether, then, you eat or drink or whatever you do, do all to the glory of God.

1 Corinthians 10:31 (NASB)

Therefore, if anyone is in Christ, he is a new creation; old things have passed away; behold, all things have become new.

2 Corinthians 5:17 (NKJV)

CHAPTER 2

Ain't No Mountain High Enough: Overcoming the Barriers

And it will be said, "Build up, build up, prepare the way, remove every obstacle out of the way of My people."
Isaiah 57:14 (NASB)

B y now we know that proper nutrition habits and lifestyle choices are the keys to achieving and maintaining overall health and wellness. But let's be honest. For some, adopting these habits can be inherently difficult. There may be some barriers beyond your control that exist as you begin your quest for health.

In an attempt to change nutritional habits and opt for healthy food choices, you may find yourself in an area plagued with limited resources. There is no denying that some neighborhoods are blanketed with fast food restaurants selling mostly foods with high fat, high salt, and low nutritional value. When talking with some patients about making healthier choices, the usual response is "I don't have access to that type of food," or "Healthy food is too expensive." "Food deserts," or areas with a limited availability of fresh fruits, vegetables and whole-grains, can prove to be real obstacles for those looking to make healthy diet choices.

Some might be facing financial challenges and thinking that starting an exercise regimen is beyond your reach. There is no extra room in the budget for a gym membership, a personal trainer, or for fancy equipment to set up a home gym, so fitness simply isn't an option.

While these are all valid barriers, there are ways

to overcome them and reach all of your necessary health and wellness goals in spite of limited resources.

Less frills, more deals

Believe it or not, we can have access to healthier foods. In most urban communities there is usually a no-frill, inexpensive chain grocery store that can supply all of your healthy food choices. These stores are usually less expensive than the traditional chain supermarkets due to, as they say "no-frills;" no fancy marketing, no big displays, and no focus on brand-name products. Just shelves, coolers, and food. But, the healthy food choices are there!

- **Look for the higher quality products**. When in these stores they may read Grade A, Fancy, or Superior.

- **Watch for sales. S**ign up for email alerts so you can plan your grocery trip in advance and plan your meals around the foods items on sale for the week.

- **Buy fresh produce**. Always buy fresh if possible. If not, buy frozen. Frozen veggies are picked and then frozen at peak ripeness when the nutritional value is at its highest. This can make frozen goods a better value while being edible for months longer. Canned goods tend to have more salt and preservatives and therefore, don't make the best first choice.

Plan a menu

This is the step that most people miss. You have to plan your grocery trips in order to make them efficient and effective. It's best to make your purchases as planned healthy meals. Making a list and sticking to it helps you to buy only the healthy things you planned to buy and avoid the impulse "less than healthy" buys.

For example, tonight's dinner could be salmon, with brown rice and sautéed spinach. For this dish, in addition to your seasonings and spices, there are just 3 grocery items that need to make it to the list - salmon, brown rice, and spinach. This approach will help guide you in the store and hopefully prevent overspending and buying what you don't need.

Don't be fooled

Don't ever think that the grocery stores aren't designed for you to spend your money - and lots of it! The very layout of the average large chain grocery store is intended to captivate your senses and cause you to buy impulsively. Unfortunately, the impulse buys aren't always the healthiest.

However, if you prefer the larger chain grocery stores, there are some tricks to shopping in these stores as well.

- **Shop the perimeter**. All of the fresh fruit and veggies, dairy and meat selections are typically along the walls of the supermarket. When you start heading down the aisles, you are headed toward trouble...chips, cookies, and processed foods.

- **If it's next to the register, leave it there.** Most likely a high-sugar or high-salt snack, these are the impulse buy racks. The store is hoping while you're waiting in line you'll grab a bag of chips or a candy bar. Resist the temptation.

- **Never grocery shop while hungry.** Try having a healthy snack before venturing out. This will help you avoid some common dietary pitfalls.

Pay now, save later

Oftentimes, when buying fresh foods instead of processed foods, there is a noticeable price difference. But to keep things in perspective, it is important to remember that the cost of treating chronic illnesses and diseases after a lifetime of poor nutrition choices is far more costly. While seemingly daunting at first, there are many ways to work within the parameters of your resources to incorporate healthy dietary options.

- **Stick to the script**. Fresh foods will spoil if not cooked. Therefore, you have to plan your menus ahead of time, shop for the week and stick to the script. There's nothing worse than throwing out spoiled food. It will make you less likely to buy fresh again.

- **Inquire about urban farmer's markets**. Many urban gardens and farmer's markets are cropping up, allowing access to fresh foods in areas once considered "food deserts." Many of these farmer's markets participate in subsidized programs or even accept government assistance as forms of payment.

Use the world around you

According to the Centers for Disease Control and Prevention (CDC), seven out of every ten adults in this country are overweight or obese. For African Americans, these numbers are even more staggering. For black men, 70% are overweight or obese, while 82% of black women fall into this category. The reason...we simply aren't moving enough. In fact, it is estimated that less than 20% of us report that we participate in "regular" exercise.

The most common reasons we hear as physicians as to why more people aren't exercising is that gyms, trainers, and equipment are just too expensive. We are crushing the myth that it is too expensive to exercise with practical ways you can use the world around you and start today!

- **Walk it out.** This is something that we all can do anytime, anywhere, and doesn't require any extra equipment other than what God gave you. Make it a family affair and go for walks together after dinner to help burn off those calories. It is estimated that 10,000 steps per day is optimal for maintaining good health and weight. You could invest in an inexpensive pedometer to measure every step and make sure you are hitting that 10,000 step mark each day.

- **Make your housework a workout.** Mowing the lawn, raking the leaves, or shoveling the snow can all be great forms of exercise. Even indoor activities such as vacuuming, mopping, and scrubbing can count as exercise. The good news is that it doesn't cost a thing and has to be done anyway, so why not make it intentional?

- **Play with your kids.** Obesity is not just a problem amongst our adults, but our kids are affected as well. In fact, in the African American community, it's estimated that 40% of children are overweight or obese. They grow up to become overweight or obese adults. We've got to break the cycle. Join them in playing. Throw and catch a ball, play tag, walk them to the park, and watch your family's fitness level improve. This is an often underrated yet simple way to incorporate fitness into your day.

- **Play with *your* toys.** We had to include this one for the guys. We know a lot of you out there are gamers, and we also know that a lot of wives fuss at their men for being addicted to video games. Why not compromise and choose those games that allow you to be a part of the action as opposed to just watching it? There are several games on the market that allow you to train like a professional athlete, compete in an Olympic sport, or workout with a trainer. This is a win-win, where you never have to worry about defending your gaming time again.

- **Improvise.** You don't have to spend a penny on exercise equipment. You can use ordinary household items for various upper and lower body exercises. Canned goods, water bottles, back packs filled with books, can all be used for weight training and building strength.

It is vital as Christians that we remove these barriers that keep us in sickness and start seeking good health. As believers, we all have a divine purpose to fulfill. How can we possibly continue to be effective in the body of Christ, when our own bodies are unhealthy? We must be in our best shape, physically, in order to be at our best for God's service.

The family that prays together...

God, we thank you for revealing to us the barriers in our minds and in our lives that have been preventing us from living our best and healthiest lives. We will no longer let anything stop us from achieving the best health that you desire for us.

Move any mountains or obstacles that may be in our way. Allow us to be resourceful and creative in using what you have given us. Help us to find new ways to get active and open our eyes to the endless possibilities of eating a healthy diet.

As you continue to enhance our lives, help us to be agents of change within our families, churches, and communities. As we come to understand your will for us to live a healthy life, help us to share the message with others.

Help us to support one another, believe in one

another, and pray for one another to reach the goals

we have set. In Jesus' powerful name, Amen,

WORD to live by...

And it will be said,
"Build up, build up, prepare the way,
Remove every obstacle out of the way of My people."
Isaiah 57:14 (NASB)

But my God shall supply all your need according to
his riches in glory by Christ Jesus.
Philippians 4:19 (KJV)

Then Jesus told them, "I tell you the truth, if you have
faith and don't doubt, you can do things like this and
much more. You can even say to this mountain, 'May
you be lifted up and thrown into the sea,' and it will
happen.
Matthew 21:21 (NLT)

Now all glory to God, who is able, through his
mighty power at work within us, to accomplish
infinitely more than we might ask or think.
Ephesians 3:20 (NLT)

CHAPTER 3

YOUR HEALTH IS YOUR WEALTH

Beloved, I wish above all things that thou mayest prosper and be in health, even as thy soul prospereth.
3 John 1:2 (KJV)

Many have heard the expression "your health is your wealth," but few actually grasp the depth of this statement. This is not all that surprising in the Christian community given the opposing views that exist within the Church as it relates to money. There's a debate about whether tithing is still applicable. There's a debate about whether or not we should be financially successful. There's even a debate about whether or not church leaders should be compensated. Consequently, as

Christians, we are often left feeling uncomfortable talking about money.

Regardless of your personal beliefs concerning wealth and who should strive for it, we challenge you to see an often overlooked principle: ***Your health is your wealth***. It's your most important asset and commodity. Without good health you're unable to live in purpose, accomplish your goals, and do all of the things you have been called to do.

With many in the Christian community being uncomfortable talking about "money" and the biblical principles behind it, we can see why this correlation to our health is not very well understood. But 3 John 1:2 tells us that health and wealth go hand in hand.

Beloved, I wish above all things that thou mayest prosper and be in health, even as thy soul prospereth.

In the text we see Paul writing his desire that we

would *prosper* AND be in *good health*. This implies that we certainly shouldn't strive to have one without the other, but that achieving both is possible. He goes on to make the statement that we should have the same urgency in achieving prosperity and healthy bodies as we do for our souls being healthy and prosperous. The takeaway: **we are to be whole...in *every* area**.

Here are some gentle reminders to help you and your spouse to remember that even in the most practical sense your health is your wealth. Strive to prosper in both, just as your soul prospers!

Your health is your most important asset.

What can be of more value than our very own lives? 1 Corinthians 6:19-20 (NIV) reminds us that we were bought with a price. Therefore, we are to honor God with our bodies.

"Do you not know that your bodies are temples of the Holy Spirit, who is in you, whom you have received from God? You are not your own; you were bought at a price. Therefore honor God with your bodies."

Just think of how valuable you are in the Lord's eyes. Let's put on the mind of Christ and view ourselves in that same light. Let's value ourselves enough to keep our bodies in great working condition. Let's value ourselves enough to make sure we are having regular visits with the doctor to detect health issues before they develop or when they are in their earliest stages. Let's value ourselves enough to talk about health issues in the family that have previously been taboo. The Lord spared nothing in his purchase of us, so why not invest in your health as if your life depends on it...because it does!

Time is of the essence.

Oftentimes, we may decide that we don't have time to make our health a priority. With rigorous family demands, ministry demands, and the occasional leisurely demands we don't seem to have enough hours in the day.

But let's be honest with ourselves. We certainly seem to make time for the things that are important to us. Somehow we just seem to forget the biblical mandate that our health *is* supposed to be important to us too.

Time is of the essence as it relates to your health. If you delay investing the time needed to maintain your health now, you may find yourself investing a lot more time recuperating later.

Let's look at an example of an adult beginning at age 21 over the course of 59 years (using an average life expectancy of 80 years):

Health maintenance/Prevention

1 doctor's visit for 1 hour each year:

1 hour x 59 years = 59 hours per lifetime

Maintenance of chronic medical condition

1 doctor's visit 4 times per year:

1 hour x 4 times per year x 59 years = 196 hours per lifetime

Maintenance of a chronic medical condition with complications

Example: uncontrolled HTN --> chronic kidney disease--> dialysis

1 doctor's visit 12 times per year:

1 hour x 12 times per year x 59 years = 708 hours per lifetime

In addition to...

Dialysis for 4 hours, 3 days per week:

4 hours x 156 times per year x 59 years = 9,204 hours per lifetime

Grand total: 708 hours + 9,204 hours = 9,912 hours per lifetime

As you can see, the minor investment in time now, can lead to a vast amount of time saved over the course of your lifetime.

You can't afford NOT to invest in your health.

High copays and deductibles and lacking vacation time or sick days shouldn't be the issue that keeps you from the doctor or taking care of your health. Oftentimes, our first excuse for not making appointments is that "I just don't have the time off," or "I don't get paid leave from work."

At first glance, these certainly seem like valid reasons to make sure you make it to your 9-to-5 daily. However, think of the consequences of poor health.

You won't be able to go to that job or provide for your family if health issues cause you to be disabled or cause premature death.

Another common excuse is that it is just too expensive to go to the doctor. That copay may be a sacrifice, but the cost of treating a condition diagnosed in its advanced stages simply because it was ignored can be huge. You can only imagine how much 9,912 hours of care for chronic kidney disease and dialysis would cost! Make the sacrifice now to preserve your wealth later.

The earlier, the better.

It's no secret that illnesses are more expensive to treat when in more advanced stages as opposed to when the illness is caught early or even prevented. Routine preventative care can save tons in the long run.

Let's look at our same example. Untreated high blood pressure can lead to kidney failure and a lifetime of expensive dialysis treatments. The cost of a $75 copay or a $200 self-pay to visit the doctor pales in comparison to a paying for a lifetime of dialysis treatments.

Making the small investment of money to find out you need to make lifestyle adjustments in order to prevent high blood pressure is nothing compared to the potential cost of a lifetime of consequences. Make the effort to invest in your health now and avoid those preventable health issues later.

The family that prays together...

God, we thank you for loving us unconditionally. We thank you for the revelation of just how important we are to you. Father, you bought us with a price, and for that we are truly grateful.

We take on the mind of Christ and see ourselves as the wonderful creations you made us to be. Thank you for reminding us that our bodies are not our own and we are to honor you with our very lives.

Help us to always be proactive as it relates to our health and to remember the value that our lives have to our families, our communities, and to the Kingdom.

Lord, we know that it is your will that we would prosper and be in good health. Thank you for giving us the tools we need to prosper in every area of our lives including our health.

Help us to support one another, believe in one

another, and pray for one another to reach the goals we have set.

In Jesus' unsurpassable name, Amen.

WORD to live by...

Beloved, I wish above all things that thou mayest prosper and be in health, even as thy soul prospereth.
3 John 1:2 (KJV)

Do you not know that your bodies are temples of the Holy Spirit, who is in you, whom you have received from God? You are not your own; you were bought at a price. Therefore honor God with your bodies.
1 Corinthians 6:19-20 (NIV)

I will give thanks to You, for I am fearfully and wonderfully made; Wonderful are Your works, And my soul knows it very well.
Psalm 139:14 (NASB)

We have come to know and have believed the love which God has for us. God is love, and the one who abides in love abides in God, and God abides in him.
1 John 4:16 (NASB)

CHAPTER 4

HEAD OF THE HOUSEHOLD:
MEN'S HEALTH MATTERS

Husbands, love your wives, just as Christ loved the church and gave himself up for her.
Ephesians 5:25 (NIV)

As the head of the household, men often feel as though it is their responsibility to provide, protect, and to lead. We are committed to faith, family, and making power moves in life. Many of us hold true to the principles outlined in Ephesians 5:21-33 and love our wives and would do anything for them. But when it comes to viewing our health as the main threat to fulfilling this role, we tend to miss the connection. Keeping ourselves healthy enough to live a lifetime with our wives could easily be viewed as the ultimate expression of love.

So often I am asked, "What is the biggest health threat facing our men today?" Initially you may think it is diabetes, or high blood pressure, or maybe even heart disease, but my reply to this question is always the same, "indifference." As leaders in our home, church, and community, we make it our business to be strong, fearless, reliable, and knowledgeable as we aim to lead by example. However, when it comes to our health, as men, we are often vulnerable, filled with fear, uncommitted, and indifferent.

Revelation 3:19 (NLT) warns us against being indifferent in our spiritual health.

I correct and discipline everyone I love. So be diligent and turn from your indifference.

We should take the same stance in matters of our physical health. We often don't realize that we are unhealthy and we are indifferent to the fact that our bodies are the temple of the Holy Spirit and should be treated as such.

This isn't a new phenomenon. In fact, the Apostle Paul advises us against indifference towards our maintaining our bodies. He reminds us just how sacred our bodies really are in 1 Corinthians 6:19-20 (NLT).

Don't you realize that your body is the temple of the Holy Spirit, who lives in you and was given to you by God? You do not belong to yourself, for God bought you with a high price. So you must honor God with your body.

Studies have shown that men are three times less likely than women to go to a doctor when suffering from similar symptoms. It should then be no surprise that men also have shorter average life expectancies. Year after year, as these statistics are reported, it is shown that men are no more invested in their health now than they were decades ago.

As men we take pride in our strength, our ability to provide, and to be the head of our household, yet we disregard the one element that is most instrumental in attaining and maintaining this - our health. While it is evident that our health as men should be a priority, there are still some of us who simply *choose* not to participate in our own health care.

So what is it that keeps up from going to the doctor?

The Mechanic Phenomena

Many men view the doctor in much the same way they view an auto-mechanic. I often hear, "I would go to the doctor but I know they're just going to find something wrong. Just like when I go to the car dealership and all I want is an oil change, and they tell me I need hundreds of dollars of service." After hearing this sentiment time and time again, I began to find this response disheartening, yet brutally honest.

Unfortunately, there appears to be a general perception that doctors desire to diagnose their patients with a multitude of issues in hopes that this will result in more visits and increased revenue. This is just like the perception that auto-mechanics tend to inflate the services needed when seeking repairs. While I won't deny that there may be some physicians that are motivated by something other than solely the patient's best interests, you have to understand that this is not the norm.

Let's try and keep this in perspective. Just because you have encountered auto-mechanics or other service men that may try to make you pay for unnecessary services, do you stop seeking repairs on your car? Or do you take the position of knowing as much as you can about your car ahead of time to ensure that you're not bamboozled the next time you take your car to the shop for repairs?

Why not take the same approach to your health? You are your own best advocate for your health and we all need to take the time to learn as much as we can about it. Similarly, you engage in regular maintenance and routine checkups to ensure your car is working properly. Why not take the same preventative approach to your health?

Oil changes, air filters, brake and tire maintenance, all go with car ownership. However, some choose to ignore the advice the mechanic gives for regular maintenance. Unfortunately, this often proves costly as the car ages without being maintained and the related damages and associated repairs end up being more expensive than the preventive maintenance that was offered months ago.

In the same manner, many ignore the advice of their physician and take on the "if it ain't broke, don't fix it" mentality. The problem is that after years of neglect, your health can deteriorate leaving you facing a lifetime of chronic disease. It is important to remember that preventive health maintenance helps to avoid chronic illness and/or detect it in its earliest stages, saving you time and money in the long run. It is far more difficult and expensive to treat a chronic medical condition and its consequences than it is to prevent it altogether.

Equip yourself with information to have informed discussions with your doctor. Try to go to an appointment, not just when the engine starts knocking or when lights on the console start blinking, but when everything is running smoothly. This will ensure you receive the preventative maintenance you need to maintain your good health.

No One Told Me

It's no secret that women are encouraged to become active participants in their health from the onset of puberty. As young women begin to go through changes including the onset of their menstrual cycle and breast development, gynecological exams and other routine health screenings give them reason to continue to seek medical care. Due to this constant engagement with the health care system a woman begins to recognize going to the doctor as "the norm," and therefore, doesn't shy away from the experience.

In stark contrast, as young men we aren't given a roadmap to follow that guides us through our healthcare. Men are not given any instructions on when to see their doctor or what health ailments we need to be on the lookout for during our adolescent and young adult years. I blame the healthcare community in large part for this as we have not made a conscious effort to engage men.

In my conversations, I have found that most men in their 30's - 40's had their last interaction with a physician at or about the time they were entering college. There is a huge gap between obtaining our physical exam for entrance into college to having your first prostate exam around age 40. More often than not, unless a man is a college or professional athlete undergoing routine physicals for participation in a sport, then there's a good chance that no one is encouraging him to seek medical attention for routine health maintenance.

This lack of familiarity with seeking routine medical care leads to a lack of understanding of the importance of preventative health maintenance and a fundamental under appreciation for the need to maintain one's health. Furthermore, it perpetuates the misbelief that we don't *need* to go to the doctor unless we are sick. Consequently, we end up missing the opportunity to "maintain" our health. Instead of being *proactive* we end up taking a *reactive* approach to our healthcare, only seeking medical attention when we become ill; and oftentimes, not until it is too late.

Ain't Nobody Got Time For That

Another common reason that men give for not seeing their healthcare provider on a regular basis is that they simply don't have time. Between working long hours, caring for their families, and trying to find time to enjoy leisure activities; they just can't seem to find time to go to the doctor. These increasing demands have resulted in very little time to fit more "stuff" into our daily schedules.

What I find interesting is that we seem to make time for everything *except* investing in our health. We make time for the things that are important to us. Whether it's making modifications to our favorite sports car, attending sporting events, gaming online, shooting pool, or having a weekly card game with friends; if we view it as important, we find time to do it.

I believe that your health is the most important asset you have and I encourage you to take on a similar mindset. If we truly value ourselves, our families, and our friends, we will do what is necessary to ensure that we are around to celebrate life with those very people that we care about. This can only be accomplished if we maintain our health!

What I try to impress upon men is that when you take a proactive, preventative approach to your health, you typically only have to see your doctor 1-2 times per year! This is a relatively small percentage of your time when you consider the benefits that those visits have on your health and well-being.

Many say they can't sacrifice the "sick time" off from work. The fact is that the very job that is allowing you to provide for your family, the family that you enjoy spending time with, and the activities that you participate in, mean little or nothing if you're not around to enjoy them. Add chronic disease treatments and maintenance to the equation and you will need a lot more time off.

The will of God is for us to be just as healthy physically, as we are spiritually. In 3 John 1:2, the

Apostle John eludes to a key parallel between our spiritual and physical health. This chart illustrates the similarities between our physical and spiritual health.

	Spiritual Health	Physical Health
Checkups Needed	✓	✓
Maintenance Required	✓	✓
Training Materials Available	✓	✓
Warning Signs	✓	✓

- **Checkups Needed:** For our spiritual health to be assessed we go to church. For our physical health, we need to get checkups! What's interesting is that the vast majority of men I have encountered view themselves as "pretty healthy" or "very healthy;" however, they have no objective means of assessing their health. Specifically, most men admit to not having seen a physician within the past year and more often than not, many of them have not seen a doctor in the past several years. So how do you *know* you're healthy?

- **Maintenance Required:** For our spiritual health, we should feed and nourish our souls daily with the Word. Likewise, for our physical health, we have to feed and nourish our bodies daily with healthy foods, fruits, vegetables, and the fuel for life.

- **Training Materials Available:** For our spiritual health, we have to study to show ourselves approved. (2 Timothy 2:15) For our physical health there's nothing wrong with taking the time to learn what it means to be healthy. For many, this is a new concept and a lifestyle adjustment. As a result, you may have to do some research and discover information which will help you live your best and healthiest life. This book is a great start!

- **Warning Signs:** For our spiritual health we all have to be obedient to the call of the Holy Spirit and use our discernment wisely. With the indwelling of His spirit we have an immediate alarm when things aren't quite right and aren't in agreement with His spirit. Similarly with our physical health we have to listen to our body. That ache, pain, or never ending fatigue, may be your body telling you that something is wrong. Never ignore the signs, just as you shouldn't ignore the nudging and direction of the Holy Spirit in any other setting.

Fear

Another factor keeping men from going to the doctor is our fear that the doctor will diagnose us with some life threatening, life altering diagnosis that takes away from our manliness. Of the countless conversations I've had, one of the prevailing themes I've heard from men is that they would "rather not know" of illness than to face their mortality. This "ignorance is bliss" mentality has led to our men dying prematurely from highly preventable illnesses or suffering from complications of disease that could have been avoided with timely diagnosis and treatment.

So what is it that we as men are so afraid of when it comes to seeing our doctors? Why do we feel that illness equates to weakness? Our culture has impressed upon us that as men we don't complain, we don't verbalize our pain, and that any behavior that is contrary to this signifies weakness.

I beg to differ with this and believe that recognizing the need for help actually signifies strength. Only a strong man can admit that he doesn't have all the answers! Only a strong man will admit that he can't do it all alone. Only the strongest of men can face their fears and know that they will be victorious no matter what situation arises. Remember, fear is not of God.

For God has not given us the spirit of fear but of power and of love, and of a sound mind.
2 Timothy 1:7 (NKJV)

The family that prays together...

Lord, we thank you for being the giver of life. It is in you that we live, and move, and have our being. You came that we might have life and have it more abundantly. Thank you for the realization that abundant living comes through healthy living and for giving us the tools to do so.

As the head of our lives, we thank you for being the perfect example of love, provision, protection, and leadership. By loving you, we learn that we can love ourselves and our spouses enough to want a long, healthy, and fruitful life.

Help us not to let our past experiences dictate how we view our health. Help us to overcome any fear, indifference, or other barriers to receiving the best that you have for us as it relates to our health. Father, we seek your guidance as we start this journey toward abundant living.

Help us to support one another, believe in one another, and pray for one another to reach the goals we have set. In Jesus' matchless name, Amen.

WORD to live by...

Don't you realize that your body is the temple of the Holy Spirit, who lives in you and was given to you by God? You do not belong to yourself, 20 for God bought you with a high price. So you must honor God with your body.
1 Corinthians 6:19-20 (NLT)

For God has not given us the spirit of fear but of power and of love, and of a sound mind.
2 Timothy 1:7 (NKJV)

Brothers and sisters, I do not consider myself yet to have taken hold of it. But one thing I do: Forgetting what is behind and straining toward what is ahead
Philippians 3:13 (NIV)

For the husband is the head of the wife, as Christ also is the head of the church, He Himself being the Savior of the body.
Ephesians 5:23 (NASB)

CHAPTER 5

REST, RELEASE, RECHARGE: A WOMAN'S GUIDE TO HEALTH

And let us not be weary in well doing: for in due season we shall reap, if we faint not.
Galatians 6:9 (KJV)

Acommon health issue I see plaguing women is *burnout* - being exhausted mentally, physically, and spiritually. The unfortunate thing is that women on the verge of burnout often don't recognize the signs. It is easy to see why it so often goes unrecognized because it may present itself in a wide variety of symptoms such as increased irritability, fatigue, stomach upset, forgetfulness, insomnia, TMJ (temporomandibular joint syndrome), depression, and headaches; just to name a few. While burnout is not found solely in women, there are some unique features that speak to the very essence of why this is a common problem that women face.

Women are nurturers. God designed us this way. We nurture, serve and protect our families, friends, and loved ones. As women striving for the model left for us in Proverbs 31, we work, manage our households, provide for our families, care for our husbands and children, and are leaders in our communities. We give of ourselves "tirelessly." Or do we?

This notion that women should operate tirelessly, is a faulty one. It's unnatural, it's not biblical, and it's not healthy. Psalm 4:8 (NASB) tells us that we find peace in our sleep, because with God we can rest in safety.

In peace I will both lie down and sleep, For You alone, O Lord, make me to dwell in safety.

There is even reference to "sweet sleep" in Proverbs 3:24 (NASB).

When you lie down, you will not be afraid;
When you lie down, your sleep will be sweet.

Without a doubt, sleep is necessary for the body to grow, function, and operate appropriately. Research shows us that those with sleep deprivation suffer from fatigue, poor attention, lack of concentration, motivation, and decreased functioning during the daytime or waking hours. There are also significant physical effects. Studies have shown a link between a lack of sleep and high blood pressure, depression, anxiety, and heart disease.

Galatians 6:9 is clear. We need to protect ourselves from growing weary - even in well doing. Yes, that means we are to protect ourselves from weariness; as we serve our families, as we lead our communities, and as we give our time and talents to the work of ministry. Put simply, we need to protect our gift of womanhood.

The Caretaker Syndrome

Many women find themselves facing burnout as a result of their own gift of nurturing. Often a term used when describing someone experiencing burnout after caring for a chronically ill family member, Caretaker Syndrome is a phenomenon that many women can relate to.

In Caretaker Syndrome, the health of the caretaker has gone unchecked, leaving them prone to depression and a myriad of other health conditions. It is usually seen during the long-term care of a loved one during a chronic illness, or for end-of-life care; whether it be aging parents, a terminally ill child, spouse, or even a friend. However, anyone caring for another's needs can in theory experience this syndrome. I'm sure most new parents would agree.

The symptoms are often described as physical, emotional, and psychological exhaustion; listlessness; fatigue; a need for diversion; and a growing wish to be someplace else. "The Caregiver Survival Series" by James R. Sherman, Ph.D., lists three stages that can evolve from the Caretaker Syndrome and ultimately lead to burnout. First, *frustration* sets in. Next, *depression* can develop including prolonged periods of helplessness, loss of concentration, and control. Ultimately, *despair* leads to hopelessness and resentment.

Whether you are fulfilling the role of wife, mother, or daughter to an elderly parent, or if you are in fact charged with caring for a family member with special needs, living the life of a caregiver can be an arduous task. Their needs always come first. Your day can quickly be consumed with where they have to be, what they need to do, what they need to eat, what medicines need to be given, and every other aspect of their daily activities.

But what happens when you "just don't feel like it" that day? Is there someone who can get the task done and take care of the daily business without having to ask you questions every step of the process? What happens if you fall ill, or you just can't do it?

Yes, you are needed. Yes, you are appreciated for all you do. But have you taken the time to ensure your emotional, physical, and mental needs are being met? Do you allow others to help with your duties when needed? Oftentimes, for the caregiver the answer to these questions is "No," and it can lead to some dire consequences.

There are some practical steps that have proven to be beneficial in resolving some of these feelings encountered by those with the Caretakers Syndrome.

- **Ask for help** - Expressing your sense of exhaustion and feelings of being overwhelmed is the first step. Don't be afraid to ask for help whether it be from other family members, friends, your church, or other community resources. Now may be the time to look for outside help to provide assistance with light housekeeping or the care of your loved one so you can get out and enjoy time for yourself.

- **Write it down** - Journaling helps to resolve feelings of discontentment or at least it may help you to acknowledge hidden feelings of guilt or resentment. Being able to verbalize or put on paper your deepest thoughts helps to put your situation in perspective.

- **Talk it out** - Counseling is always an option. Just talk about it and get another point

ROBERT C. ROBINSON III, M.D. & KARLA L. ROBINSON, M.D.

of view from a pastor, doctor, social worker, or licensed counselor.

- **"Me" time** - Make time for yourself because it's imperative to your mission. If you don't take care of you, who will? It's an important question to ask.

- **Exercise** – One great way to relieve stress is to exercise. It can help to clear your mind, make you feel better, and give you energy. There are long term benefits for your body, mind, and spirit when you make exercise a part of your daily routine.

- **Groups** - Support groups can be helpful. Group settings let you interact with others who completely understand what you are experiencing and may have insight to help you cope effectively. Whether it's a wives' club, parent group, or other church/community gathering, take advantage of the fellowship.

As caregivers, remember that your mental, physical, and emotional health needs must be met first, in order for you to be efficient and effective. It's important to stay encouraged, always reminding yourself that what you are doing is noble, honorable, and necessary.

As women, we have to be careful to rest, recharge, and release the stress of nurturing that so often plagues us. This is a perpetual process. In fact, the Word tells us to renew our minds (Romans 12:2), and reminds us that we should strive to renew our inner man day by day (2 Corinthians 4:16).

Here are some tips to help you to reduce stress, renew your mind, and live a healthy life that allows you to flourish.

- **Identify your stressors.** How can you change or eliminate them if you don't know what they are? Find out what worries you, then follow the charge in 1 Peter 5:7 and cast all your cares upon Him, because He cares for you.

- **Avoid the stressors you can, change your reaction to the one's you can't.** There are some stressors that we simply can't avoid, but try not getting as worked up about them next time. Try to see God's hand in every situation...it's not easy, and takes practice, but it can be done. Remember all things work together for good for those called according to His purpose. (Romans 8:28)

- **Practice forgiveness.** Commit to ending the grudges that we carry and set the differences aside. Learn to forgive. Forgiveness is really for your benefit, not the other person. Ephesians

4:32 reminds us to forgive as Christ has forgiven us.

- **Exercise.** Having a regular exercise routine is a great stress reliever. It will help you feel better, look better, and decrease your risk of developing heart disease. Aim for a goal of at least 45 minutes per day, at least 4-5 days per week after consulting with your physician.

- **Laughter.** There is nothing wrong with unwinding and having a good time. Laughter has been shown to reduce the levels of stress hormones in the blood. Laughter really is the best medicine.

- **Be realistic when making plans.** Take charge of your schedule. Don't overcommit. Know your limits, and learn to say "no." Prioritize and do things in order of their importance. You'll be more effective and efficient for the Kingdom.

The family that prays together...

Lord, we thank you for your joy - the source of our strength. You are the author and finisher of our faith and in you we put our complete and total trust. Thank you for being a God who is concerned about what concerns us.

You would never put more on us than we could bear. Help us not to try to carry the burdens of life on our shoulders. God you are willing and able to meet our innermost needs. Help us to remember to cast all of our cares on you. Allow us to experience sweet sleep that recharges us- mind, body, and soul. Help us to release the stress that tries to overtake us. Remind us to keep ourselves healthy even when we are caring for others. Renew our minds daily and give us the strength to "not grow weary in well doing."

Help us to support one another, believe in one another, and pray for one another to reach the goals we have set. In Jesus' omnipotent name, Amen.

WORD to live by...

A cheerful heart is good medicine, but a broken spirit saps a person's strength.
Proverbs 17:22 (NLT)

And do not be conformed to this world, but be transformed by the renewing of your mind, so that you may prove what the will of God is, that which is good and acceptable and perfect.
Romans 12:2 (NASB)

Therefore we do not lose heart. Even though our outward man is perishing, yet the inward man is being renewed day by day.
2 Corinthians 4:16 (NKJV)

Instead, be kind to each other, tenderhearted, forgiving one another, just as God through Christ has forgiven you.
Ephesians 4:32 (NLT)

CHAPTER 6

LEADING BY EXAMPLE:
RAISING HEALTHY CHILDREN

Train up a child in the way he should go,
And when he is old he will not depart from it.
Proverbs 22:6 (NKJV)

B eing a parent requires sacrifice. Most of us have that moment of realization shortly after becoming parents. Our lives, as we knew them, were changed forever. Your children are now your number #1 priority. As a result, you find yourself sacrificing the personal time that you once held near and dear. Let's face it, as parents we often neglect our own needs - as our life's work is now serving others.

When we are blessed to become parents, we are blessed with the *ministry* of parenting. You might be thinking, "I'm not a minister." We challenge you to begin to think otherwise. Parenting *is* a ministry. The word *ministry* comes from the Greek word *diakoneo*, meaning "to serve, or attend to." This is exactly what we do as parents. We attend to every physical, emotional, social, and spiritual need that our children have. As a result, in most instances, as parents we are *the most* influential forces in our children's formative years. That's why we have to continuously seek God's guidance on how to parent correctly.

The scriptures are clear on the importance of using this influence to shape our children to become the best they can be. Proverbs 22:6 (NKJV) reminds us that these life lessons we impart will remain with them forever.

Train up a child in the way he should go, And when he is old he will not depart from it.

While definitely rewarding, living a life of service is certainly no small feat. In fact, one area that seems to suffer the most is our health. Those 5:00am visits to the gym have now been replaced with 5:00am feedings for our little ones, making and packing school lunches, and homework checks for our school-age kids. Instead of making grocery lists for the week and taking the time to plan our meals, we are now flying by the seat of our pants and stuck in the fast-food line most nights for dinner.

Making time for your physical health and the health of those around you can be challenging. However, it is necessary. Being a parent inherently means that you are setting the example; and excellence should always be the standard. This should include our physical health as well.

Long gone are the days of "Do as I say, not as I do." We cannot tell our children to be healthy and make healthy choices without modeling it for them. Titus 2:6-7 (NIV) helps us to understand that we are to make every effort to set the best example we can.

Similarly, encourage the young men to be self-controlled. In everything set them an example by doing what is good.

The fact of the matter is that whether we realize it or not, our children are always learning from us. Sometimes that's a great thing, and at other times...perhaps not. Therefore, our behaviors and attitudes towards lifestyle choices and nutrition that our children learn from us in the home have to be positive ones. This will go on to set a healthy framework for their adult lives.

As parents and the leaders in our home, we must challenge ourselves to remember to teach our children the importance of physical health; and bring it to the forefront of the family. By using the tips below to start building a healthy lifestyle for your family, you'll find that your children will soon be following in your footsteps.

- **Write the vision and make it plain.** Make realistic, measurable short-term health goals. You'll be more likely to stick to them and be more successful. Don't just say "I want to start exercising this year", make it a measurable goal and say "I want to start exercising 30 minutes a day, 4 days a week by the end of February." Let your children make small goals they can attain and help them celebrate the victory when they achieve it. You will all be able to build upon those short-term goals you reach in an effort to conquer the bigger ones.

- **Don't do it alone.** This principle is the very foundation of this book. When embarking on a new health and fitness routine it's important to have an accountability partner. What better partner to keep you on track than your partner in life? Your spouse knows you best and can encourage you when you get discouraged. (This WILL happen!) After making it a family affair, you can also get your church group together, , and get everyone you know on board. You're more likely to reach those goals when others are rooting for you. In 1 Thessalonians 5:11, we are reminded to encourage one another, and build one another up.

Therefore encourage one another and build up one another, just as you also are doing.

1 Thessalonians 5:11 (NASB)

- **Do it all for His glory.** We can glorify God with a healthy lifestyle, according to 1 Corinthians 10:31. Being intentional about healthy living means we can incorporate health and wellness in all that we do. We can use housework or yard work as a form of exercise as long as we get our heart rate up, we can take the stairs instead of the elevator, or simply do our praise dance just a little bit longer to get our daily exercise. Whether through a healthy diet, exercise, or simply following doctor's orders, through it all we can glorify God with better health.

Whether, then, you eat or drink or whatever you do, do all to the glory of God.

1 Corinthians 10:31 (NASB)

The family that prays together...

Lord, we thank you for reminding us that we should never be too busy to pray, just as we should never be too busy to lead a healthy lifestyle. We are intentional about making sure we are taking the time to make healthy choices for ourselves and for our children.

Help us to be better leaders in the home and to lead our children by example in all that we do. Help us to maintain order, focus, and endurance to carry out your perfect will for our lives. While we gladly serve others, help us to always remember to meet our own physical and spiritual needs.

We thank you Lord for giving us an accountability partner in our spouse. We will seek to encourage one another and continue to build one another up on this journey.

Help us to support one another, believe in one another, and pray for one another to reach the goals we have set. In Jesus' precious name, Amen.

WORD to live by...

Train up a child in the way he should go, And when he is old he will not depart from it.
Proverbs 22:6 (NKJV)

Don't let anyone look down on you because you are young, but set an example for the believers in speech, in conduct, in love, in faith and in purity.
1 Timothy 4:12 (NIV)

In the same way, let your light shine before others, that they may see your good deeds and glorify your Father in heaven.
Matthew 5:16 (NIV)

So encourage each other and build each other up, just as you are already doing.
1 Thessalonians 5:11 (NLT)

CHAPTER 7

FAITH AND MEDICINE

***For just as the body without the spirit is dead,
so also faith without works is dead.***
James 2:26 (NASB)

Often considered a controversial subject to address, there is, at times, an uncomfortable relationship between faith and medicine. We find this in the secular world and amongst the Christian community. You may have even wrestled with the concept of how faith and medicine work together. With health and the inner workings of the human body being such a scientifically based concept, we often see the *scientist* in each of us at odds with the *believer* when the miraculous happens.

The faith factor is that "inexplicable" turn of events that cause things to shift in our favor. You have seen it, and maybe you have even experienced it. Some call it being "lucky," others call it a coincidence, while a faithful believer may call it a miracle. But we have all experienced the hand of God move upon us - whether we realized it or not.

In medicine, we see it all the time. We may see a patient in the hospital that is seemingly at death's door have a miraculous recovery and be discharged home after the prayer warriors have rallied together in faith. We have also seen patients in the clinic with cancerous tumors suddenly have a normal exam and tests, after activating their faith and will to live. This is the faith factor.

Make no mistake about the fact that God certainly desires healing for His children, as evidenced by 3 John 1:2 (NASB).

Beloved, I pray that in all respects you may prosper and be in good health, just as your soul prospers.

But the question often remains, "By what means?" As physicians and ministers of the Gospel, we are in the unique position to witness the struggle that many have in answering this question first-hand.

It is not unusual for us to see faith-filled patients that haven't sought timely care for their health, or refuse to follow doctor's orders in an attempt to wait for God to manifest His healing power. Similarly, it is just as common for us to see those who feel betrayed by God or feel as though their prayers have not been answered because they have been prescribed medication, have a chronic diagnosis such as mental illness, or have to go through with a surgical procedure.

In trying to bridge the gap between faith and medicine, one thing must be understood. The power of prayer cannot be denied. Although it is difficult to quantify the outcome of prayer on health, countless research has shown prayer to be effective in the healing process. In the *Positive Therapeutic Effects of Intercessory Prayer in a Coronary Care Unit Population* study published in the Southern Medical Journal in 1988 by Dr. Randolph Byrd, the power of prayer on patients recovering from heart conditions was examined[1]. According to his research, patients receiving prayer had a better and faster recovery than those that did not receive prayer.

There are numerous examples of people being healed of various ailments through the power of prayer, defying every explanation of modern science.

This shouldn't be surprising given what the Word of God says about faith and healing in the story of the woman with the issue of blood.

> *Jesus turned and saw her. "Take heart, daughter," he said, "your faith has healed you." And the woman was healed at that moment.*
> **Matthew 9:22 (NIV)**

So does that mean we can we pray health issues away? Absolutely! But it doesn't happen that way for everyone in every circumstance. Some people do have the testimony of having a cancer diagnosis, with a visual tumor on imaging studies, only to pray and have subsequent studies show all traces of cancer are gone. There are many who had clinical and measurable hearing loss, only to have hearing restored and normal testing after praying and/or being prayed for. However, this is not everyone's story.

For some, answered prayer comes in the form of skilled physicians who can manage your complex diagnoses. For others, healing may come in the form of experimental medications that were born out of medical advancements. Or it just may manifest as the willpower to make those weight loss, exercise, and nutrition changes that can reverse high blood pressure, diabetes, and cholesterol issues.

For some in the faith community, the notion exists that if we go to the doctor, use prescription medications, or follow doctor's orders there is somehow a lack of belief that God *can* or *will* answer our prayer for healing. Or worse still, you just might be cancelling the healing work that God is doing with your "lack of faith."

There shouldn't have to be a choice. It shouldn't be that healing only takes place through *either* God and prayer *or* doctors and conventional medicine.

There is a natural synergy that exists, leading us to believe it is God *and* prayer working *with and through* doctors and conventional medicine.

Whether acknowledged or not, there is no denying the importance of the ministry of each physician and healthcare professional. We believe this is by divine design, not accident. Lest we forget the Gospel according to Luke and the book of Acts were both written by Luke, the beloved physician as he was called. (Colossians 4:14) Can we really believe that the same power Luke references in Scripture and the gifts God gave him to heal the sick are mutually exclusive and cannot coexist?

The problem exists when we choose to limit the power of prayer to only a manifestation that we desire to see. However, the power of prayer is limitless and just might take the form of physicians like us who pray before each patient encounter for God's direction and revelation. Or it may take the form of a medication that allows one to now have mental "health," or a skilled nutritionist that helps those achieve health and wellness through their diet. It may even take the form of a loving spouse that encourages you to read this book. The list can really go on and on.

While some argue that choosing to seek the help of a physician or agreeing to use medication, indicates a lack of faith in God's ability to heal, we believe it is quite the contrary. Seeking treatment from a medical professional shows that you are in fact exercising Godly wisdom in attempting to take care of your temple. Remember the words in Proverbs 4:7 (TLB).

Getting wisdom is the most important thing you can do! And with your wisdom, develop common sense and good judgment.

There is no biblical support that using medication is displaying a lack of faith. In fact, we actually see an illustration in the Bible of Jesus using "medicine" in one of His many miraculous healings.

Most often in the healing stories of Jesus, there is a touch or a Word spoken to deliver the person from their particular affliction. However, in John 9:1-8, we see a distinct difference. In this example of healing, Jesus actually makes a paste and applies it to the eyes of a man born blind. Couldn't Jesus have spoken a word of healing, or simply laid hands on the man's eyes to have them opened?

This illustration can help you understand just how God can use *anything* to deliver your healing. While we certainly believe that God can and will reverse illnesses instantly and miraculously, allow yourselves to remain open to the many possibilities in which the healing may manifest itself.

The family that prays together...

Lord, we thank you for being faithful. We thank you for being a God that not only hears but answers prayer. We are filled with faith as we think about your goodness.

God, we thank you for your healing power. We pray that you remove any sickness and disease from our bodies now as we make a commitment to maintain a healthy body and a healthy lifestyle.

While we know that it is you who heals us, we thank you for skilled and caring physicians that you have placed in our lives to guide us to a place of health and to help us maintain it. Thank you for using them as your vessels to heal your people.

Lord, while on this journey, reveal to us those areas in our lives where we are lacking faith and help us to trust and believe your Word.

Help us to support one another, believe in one another, and pray for one another to reach the goals we have set. In Jesus' incomparable name, Amen.

WORD to live by...

For just as the body without the spirit is dead, so also faith without works is dead.

James 2:26 (NASB)

And without faith it is impossible to please Him, for he who comes to God must believe that He is and that He is a rewarder of those who seek Him.

Hebrews 11:6 (NASB)

Jesus turned and saw her. "Take heart, daughter," he said, "your faith has healed you." And the woman was healed at that moment.

Matthew 9:22 (NIV)

His disciples asked him, "Rabbi, who sinned, this man or his parents, that he was born blind?" "Neither this man nor his parents sinned," said Jesus, "but this happened so that the works of God might be displayed in him.

John 9: 2-3 (NIV)

CHAPTER 8

TOO BLESSED TO BE STRESSED

Anxiety in a man's heart weighs it down,
But a good word makes it glad.
Proverbs 12:25 (NASB)

As news reports of the consequences of those living on the edge with undiagnosed or untreated mental health issues continue to flood the media, one can't help but realize that we are facing a mental health crisis in this country. Whether male or female, young or old, rich or poor, black or white, mental health issues are evident in every demographic. In this fast-paced, high stress society in which we live, it's no big surprise that the mental health of both men and women are under attack.

Just as we can find a scripture on just about any

other health concern we may be facing, the Bible also speaks about mental health and stress. This is ironic because many people with mental health challenges are viewed as having a lack of faith, or being "unchurched."

Interestingly enough, the Bible is full of examples of men and women struggling with mental health issues ranging from anxiety and depression to schizophrenia. More importantly, not all of these examples of mental illness were of people filled with demons or possessed by evil spirits. In fact, some of them were "chosen by God," but still struggling with mental health.

Many of the very issues we are facing now, many notables in the Bible faced as well. We find Moses battling low self-esteem (Exodus 3:11), self-doubt (Exodus 4:1), and anxiety about public speaking (Exodus 4:10-13). Throughout these passages, we see

Moses worried, with a ton of excuses, and afraid that he wouldn't complete the task that God has given him.

In Daniel 2:1-3, King Nebuchadnezzar is so stressed that he begins to fight insomnia, and we eventually find him displaying signs of irrational behavior. In the story of Job, we find this great man of strength displaying signs of depression, guilt, and suicidal thoughts after illness began to take over his body. (Job 3:3-7, 11)

The prophet Elijah also struggled with symptoms of depression and suicidal thoughts. In 1 Kings 19:1-5, we read how he was so exhausted and fearful while running for his life from Jezebel that depression sets in. He even cries out to God to end his life.

But living in a state of anxiety is not God's will for our lives. God gives Elijah a *prescription* to treat his feelings of despair. He tells Elijah to eat a good meal twice and then restores him to a place of peace and health. It seems God may have coined the phrase

"take two of these and call me in the morning!"

Be anxious for nothing, but in everything by prayer and supplication, with thanksgiving, let your requests be made known to God; 7 and the peace of God, which surpasses all understanding, will guard your hearts and minds through Christ Jesus.
Philippians 4:6-7 (NKJV)

As you can see; stress, worry, and anxiety, have

plagued humanity for ages. Unfortunately, some of us

have been fooled into thinking that stress is just a

normal part of our everyday lives, and have learned to

live with chronic high stress. When experiencing high

anxiety and stress levels for long periods of time, your

mental health is not only at risk, but your physical

health suffers as well.

Cortisol - a hormone that is released throughout

the body when under stress, has been linked to health

complications such as high blood sugars, poor immunity, inflammation, and heart disease just to name a few. This beneficial hormone, normally secreted to facilitate the fight-or-flight response when we are in trouble, can become detrimental to the body when continuously secreted due to chronic stress.

Find your place of peace and leave the stress behind. Your physical, emotional, and spiritual health will thank you for it. The first step in erasing stress from your life is to recognize it. Understand that much of what you've been told about stress is false. Use the truth about these common myths to help you recognize and reduce the stress you've been carrying.

- **Myth #1: Stress is normal and there is nothing we can do to prevent it.** While potentially stressful things and events are prevalent, our response to them is what determines our "stress level." We can prevent some of the stress we experience by avoiding the stressors that we can, or by changing our reaction to the stressors that we can't.

- **Myth #2: Stress shows up the same way in everyone.** This is not true. Many may have physical manifestations of their stress (physical aches and pain, abdominal pain, nausea, headaches), while others may have a more psychological manifestation (depression, anxiety, anger etc.). Every person's response to stress is different, and it may differ in the same individual depending on the stressor.

- **Myth #3: I don't have any major symptoms of stress, so I must not have it.** There can certainly be an unhealthy amount of stress before major health symptoms appear. If you are using alcohol, and/or drugs regularly, you may be self-treating stress in your life. If you are experiencing minor symptoms of stress, these may be the warning signs that things are starting to get out of control and it is the best time to reevaluate stressors in your life.

- **Myth #4: If I ignore the symptoms of stress, they will eventually go away.** Stress will not go away on its own. It takes a conscious effort by you to change the stressors in your life. Ignoring the signs of stress may lead to worsening of the manifestations of stress. Take the time to address these issues today, before it is too late.

IN SICKNESS & IN HEALTH

- **Myth #5: Stress is necessary to perform well.** This can't be further from the truth. There is a distinct difference between stress and motivation. Having goals and pushing yourself to reach them can be considered motivating factors. Anxiety, the inability to concentrate, and extreme frustration while trying to accomplish a goal is considered stress, and oftentimes leads to poor performance. For some who are still able to reach their goals under these circumstances, it is frequently in spite of stress, not because of stress.

Maintaining a stress free life requires reminding yourself that God desires better for you. There are multiple passages of Scripture that relay God's desire for you not to worry and to be at peace. Meditate on the following scriptures and follow God's plan for eliminating worry from your life.

The family that prays together...

Lord, we thank you for the revelation that some areas of our lives are filled with stress. Show us those areas of anxiety and fear that threaten our physical health and our spiritual health. Help us to cast our cares on you.

When the enemy attacks our mind, give us the strength not to be ashamed to seek help, and remind us to be open to receiving the help that we need. Help us to remember that you desire more for us to be in your perfect peace.

God, help us to keep our minds stayed on you, your promises, and your faithfulness. With you on our side, who shall we fear? When you are for us, no one can stand against us. We take comfort in your Word and it gives us peace.

Help us to support one another, believe in one

another, and pray for one another to reach the goals

we have set. In Jesus' precious name, Amen.

WORD to live by...

Peace I leave with you; My peace I give to you; not as the world gives do I give to you. Do not let your heart be troubled, nor let it be fearful.
John 14:27 (NASB)

Finally, brethren, whatever is true, whatever is honorable, whatever is right, whatever is pure, whatever is lovely, whatever is of good repute, if there is any excellence and if anything worthy of praise, dwell on these things. 9 The things you have learned and received and heard and seen in me, practice these things, and the God of peace will be with you.
Philippians 4:8-9 (NASB)

Cast all your anxiety on him because he cares for you.
1 Peter 5:7 (NIV)

Why are you in despair, O my soul?
And why have you become disturbed within
me? Hope in God, for I shall yet praise Him,
The help of my countenance and my God.
Psalm 42:11 (NASB)

CHAPTER 9

FIT TO WIN

***I discipline my body like an athlete, training
it to do what it should...***
1 Corinthians 9:27a (NLT)

We live in what many describe as a "microwave society." We want what we want, when we want it, and most often that means *now*. As a society, we have lost sight of what it means to work towards a goal and instead expect immediate results and instant gratification.

It is easy to have the mindset that if I can't have it now, I would much rather do without it. Many times we believe that we simply don't have the time to wait or go through the process. Unfortunately, and too often, this mentality is applied to every area of our lives, including our health.

When asked if good health is a priority, most people would overwhelmingly indicate they have a desire to lead healthier lives. But the fact of the matter is that while many have a desire to be healthy, most don't want to commit to the sacrifices and the time that it takes to do so.

According to the U.S. Department of Agriculture's *Dietary Guidelines for Americans, 2010,* less than 5% of adults participate in 30 minutes of physical activity each day. So while many want a healthy lifestyle, there is clearly a disconnection between what we desire and what we are willing to do to fulfill our heart's desires. A familiar passage of scripture, found in James 2:17, reminds us "faith without works is dead." Likewise, wanting a healthy lifestyle without taking the steps to achieve it is fruitless.

Seeing the importance of regular exercise in achieving optimal health can be difficult in our present culture. We live in a time where companies and advertisers offer "miracle" pills that guarantee weight loss and other health benefits, it's easy to see how someone could be convinced that exercise and an active lifestyle are no longer a necessary requirement to achieve these goals. After all, wouldn't most of us rather take a pill that claims to burn fat effortlessly then take the time to exercise?

Let's face it. There is no substitute for a good diet and a healthy exercise regimen. In actuality, they also have to be done together. You can't "out exercise" a bad diet. Similarly, you can't "out eat" a lifestyle with no exercise. It just doesn't work. In order to achieve and maintain a healthy weight and lower your risk for chronic disease, you must have a well-balanced diet *and* regular exercise regimen working together.

One of the most common reasons people give for not exercising is that they "just don't have the time." While there may not be a lot of time, fitness has to be a priority in our day in spite of our busy lives. As a busy couple, you may just have to be a little creative to incorporate exercise into your hectic schedule.

We're all aware of the importance of "date night" for couples in terms of maintaining intimacy and staying connected. But have you ever considered that making a date or appointment to exercise with your spouse might be just as important? Studies have shown that we are more successful with our exercise regimens when we have an accountability partner to keep us on track. Who better than your spouse to be that motivating factor to keep you on the road to success?

As long as you remember that you are in it for the long haul, you are sure to be successful. Recognize that despite the many false claims, achieving health is a process not an event. Being "healthy" is a lifestyle and it is going to take some time to reach your health goals and maintain them.

When discussing the importance of physical health and exercise amongst some in the faith community, we've been told "God is not concerned with my physical appearance, it's my heart that He wants." Although we agree that God wants your heart, He is also concerned that you prosper in *all* things, including your physical health. Contrary to popular belief, God's concern for the health and maintenance of your physical body can be supported by scripture.

Beloved, I pray that you may prosper in all things and be in health, just as your soul prospers.
3 John 1:2 (NKJV)

Don't you realize that your body is the temple of the Holy Spirit, who lives in you and was given to you by God? You do not belong to yourself, ²⁰ for God bought you with a high price. So you must honor God with your body.

1 Corinthians 6:19-20 (NLT)

While this latter passage in context is addressing the need to flee from sexual immorality, which is also a physical and spiritual health hazard, what we can take away from these scriptures is that we have a responsibility to honor God with our bodies and not to abuse them in *any* manner. This certainly includes the abuse that comes through neglect and poor maintenance.

In 1 Corinthians 9:27, Paul draws an interesting parallel between the importance of being "fit" for the

Kingdom physically and being "fit" for the Kingdom spiritually.

Like an athlete I punish my body, treating it roughly, training it to do what it should, not what it wants to. Otherwise I fear that after enlisting others for the race, I myself might be declared unfit and ordered to stand aside.
1 Corinthians 9:27 (TLB)

While he is referring to running the "Christian race," there is a clear message he is sending regarding the necessity of being both physically and spiritually fit. Paul reminds us of the need to train our bodies with intensity like an athlete. This is a key point. Most of us are familiar with the discipline and regimented lifestyle that any athlete needs in order to be successful in their sport. This discipline is also necessary for most of us to conquer the natural inclination we all have to do what we *want* to do, not what we *should* do.

In the spiritual sense, we can understand the need for putting our fleshly desires under subjection in order to live a holy life and not a life full of sin. (Romans 8:13) Therefore, we *train* ourselves to flee from sin, resist temptation and to crave God. It's the same principle for our physical health. We have to put unhealthy desires under subjection in order to live a healthy life as opposed to a life full of sickness. We have to *train* not to overeat, to crave exercise, and to enjoy a diet full of foods that are good for us. We have to *train* ourselves to do what we should.

The family that prays together...

God, thank you for reminding us how important it is to go through the process. Help us to understand that training, endurance, and commitment are all needed to achieve and maintain a healthy lifestyle. Thank you Lord for assuring us that all things are possible with you.

Father, we want to be fit physically and spiritually for your Kingdom. As we go to witness to others, we want to be able to share our testimony of how you changed our lives completely - physically, emotionally and spiritually!

Help us to remain consistent as we change our lifestyle to incorporate more exercise. We pray against discouragement and feeling as if our goals are not within our reach. Lord, help us to celebrate the tiny steps toward health as we continue to build towards our goals. Help us to support one another, believe in one another, and pray for one another to reach the

goals we have set. In Jesus' holy name, Amen.

WORD to live by...

Therefore I urge you, brethren, by the mercies of God, to present your bodies a living and holy sacrifice, acceptable to God, which is your spiritual service of worship.
Romans 12:1 (NASB)

She girds herself with strength,
And strengthens her arms.
Proverbs 31:17 (NKJV)

I don't know about you, but I'm running hard for the finish line. I'm giving it everything I've got. No sloppy living for me! I'm staying alert and in top condition...
1 Corinthians 9:26-27 (MSG)

Therefore, since we are surrounded by such a huge crowd of witnesses to the life of faith, let us strip off every weight that slows us down, especially the sin that so easily trips us up. And let us run with endurance the race God has set before us.
Hebrews 12:1(NLT)